Georgianna Larson, R.N., P.N.P., M.P.H. and Judith A. Kahn, M.S.W.

Special Needs Special Solutions

HOW TO GET QUALITY CARE FOR *A Child* WITH SPECIAL HEALTH NEEDS

A Guide To Health Services And How To Pay For Them

Lifeline Press

About This Book

This book represents the joint efforts of Pathfinder Resources and the Coalition for Children with Special Needs.

Copyright © 1990 Pathfinder Resources, Inc.
2324 University Avenue West, Suite 105
St. Paul, MN 55114

Published by Lifeline Press (a division of The Hohman Group, Inc.)
Printed by Anderberg/Lund Printing, Minneapolis, MN.

For additional copies write to: Lifeline Press
2500 University Avenue West
St. Paul, MN 55114

Bulk purchase discounts available. Please inquire (612-659-9114).

ISBN 0-9629995-0-4

About Pathfinder

Pathfinder Resources, Inc. is a non-profit organization that works to promote the health and well being of children and adults with chronic health conditions. Pathfinder seeks to improve existing services and to make consumers, families and professionals aware of the range of options available.

Pathfinder's mission is to bring together parents, consumers, health care providers, educators, social service professionals, third party payers and other interested parties to discuss common concerns and to coordinate the development of responses to those issues.

Acknowledgements

Special thanks go to the following people whose help made this book possible:

Douglas Toft • Copy Editor
Carol Hurgarten • Managing Editor
John Townsend • Page design and typesetting
Kathy A. Tyler • Illustrations

To everyone who worked on the book—reviewers, resource people and especially families—thanks for so many things. Your dedication to getting the word out made this all possible.

Georgianna Larson, R.N., P.N.P., M.P.H.
President and Executive Director
Pathfinder Resources, Inc.

Table

Of

Contents

Part 2 / Paying For Your Child's Care

Part 3 / Where To Find More Help

Part 4 / Special Resources For Your Child

Introduction

If your child has a disability or chronic illness, this book is for you. In the past, you've probably asked many questions about your child. When we talk to parents like you, some questions come up often: How can I get the best health care for my child? How do I pay for it? How can I take care of myself and deal with my own feelings? In this book, you'll find some answers.

Parents of children with special needs are alike in many ways. Often these parents oversee most of the care for their children. More than any doctor, they're involved with the child's care every day. For these reasons, the parents and children become the "experts" on the child's care.

As a parent, you're the key adult in your child's life. You keep track of the doctor visits, medicine, and other services your child needs. You keep records, make decisions and see the big picture. You're the person who sees how all the "pieces" of your child's care fit together.

We hope this book will help you be a skilled advocate for your child. That means knowing how to ask for the best health care. You don't have to be an expert to use our ideas. Many of them you can start using today.

At Pathfinder Resources, our work is to help improve the care of children with special health needs. We do this through workshops, networking, publishing, and advocating for better laws. In doing these things, we talk to many parents of children with various chronic health conditions, such as diabetes, asthma, epilepsy, or emotional disorders. Others have a hearing impairment, cystic fibrosis, or spina bifida. These are just a few of the conditions the children live with.

We know these parents and children make many decisions about health care. Decisions that affect their lives for many years. We asked them about the most important things they've learned and what advice they had for other parents. Many of the responses are represented in this book.

This book can't replace a personal visit with you. But it can give you facts and suggestions. We can raise common issues, and hope to help you avoid some common problems. Our goal is helping parents be more confident as they work with the health care system. We'd like them to know what the options are and how to ask for them. Parents, doctors, nurses and therapists working together as a team leads to more understanding and better care.

When we say "you" in this book, we mean parents, guardians, and anyone else caring for children with special health needs. We hope doctors, nurses, and therapists will use this book too.

What This Book Covers

◆ How to get the best health care for your child

First, this book offers ideas on finding and using services for children. Second, we discuss assertiveness skills and describe how to talk to doctors and other people in health care. The goal is to make sure everyone works together in providing the best care for your child.

◆ Ideas for working with your own feelings

Parents of children with special needs can feel a variety of emotions, including anger, guilt, or frustration, grief and sadness. It takes a lot of energy and patience to work with doctors, hospitals, therapy, school, and insurance. At times parents just feel worn out.

These feelings are normal. It helps to know that other parents go through the same things. In this book, we suggest some ideas for taking care of yourself.

◆ Paying for your child's health care

Health insurance options can seem complex. Parents may sometimes be uncertain where to turn when money is an issue.

There are many options for paying for children's health care. If necessary, parents may be able to combine these options when paying the medical bills. This book lists many programs and explains how they might work for you. It also suggests what to do when your health plan does not offer all the services your child requires.

Note: In this book, "health plan" refers to any source that pays for medical care. That might be private insurance, a health maintenance organization (HMO), Medicaid, or any other source of funds.

◆ Where to go for further help

This book will give you a place to start. On page 61, you'll find lists of materials and national organizations and agencies. They can give you many more ideas.

◆ A glossary

Beginning on page 72, you'll find a list of the important words used in this book and what they mean.

◆ Special resources for your child

Starting on page 81, we offer some suggestions on how to use your local and state resources to help provide quality care for your child. We also provide some ideas for those families without a health plan and give a list of state programs for children with special health care needs.

PART 1 / Some Basic Guidelines For Your Child's Care

CHAPTER 1 / Working With Your Health Care Team

Because your child has special health care needs, you will need to know how to work with your health care team. That team may include doctors, nurses, therapists, counselors, and others. You and your child are important members of this team. In this chapter, we suggest how you can all work together for your child's care.

Ask For A Definite Diagnosis

In many cases, disabilities are clear: The diagnosis comes at birth or time of injury. In other cases, a parent feels that something is wrong but is not sure what. Some children never have a definite diagnosis, but only a blend of symptoms and problems. In these cases, doctors may not be able to give a diagnosis. This can be hard on parents.

Some parents find it difficult to admit that their child has a chronic illness or disability. Often these conditions last a lifetime. They might call for extra care, higher costs, and more energy from parents. It's easy to see why parents may avoid a diagnosis.

Sometimes there are good reasons to wait before getting a diagnosis. This allows more time to observe and assess the child's condition. On the other hand, it can be useful to have a diagnosis. Keep in mind a diagnosis is more than just a label. Instead, the diagnosis provides an idea about how your child will grow, develop, and learn. Having a diagnosis can cut down on confusion. Many people feel better when they find a name for their child's condition: It seems less of a mystery, and they know what actions to take. Also, having a diagnosis makes it easier for some children to get services they need.

There's much to think about when asking for a diagnosis. Some things to consider are:

- *Having a diagnosis can help your child get needed services sooner. For example, a child might be helped by speech therapy, glasses, or hearing aids. Doing so can prevent problems in school. Advice to "wait and see" could delay such important help. Some services are available only with a diagnosis.*

- *A diagnosis may help the family. With a diagnosis, parents know more about the kind of behavior to expect. Without a diagnosis, it's harder for the family to set rules for behavior or help the child. Having a diagnosis also allows parents to gain skills in working with the child. For example, parents can learn sign language if their child has a hearing impairment.*

- *Doctors may decide not to give a diagnosis, not wanting a label attached to the child. They may feel it will be hard to get rid of the label later, or the problem may disappear as the child gets older.*

Is the lack of a diagnosis hard on you? Do you feel that your doctor is delaying a diagnosis to avoid upsetting you? If you answer "yes" to these questions, then clear the air. Talk to your child's doctor about this as soon as possible. Keep asking about a diagnosis until you get an answer that satisfies you.

As you talk to your doctor, state your feelings without accusing anyone. Statements like these sound blaming:

- *"You're dragging your heels."*

- *"Why are you making it so hard on us?"*

Most people will respond better if you say something like:

- *"I'm worried about not getting a diagnosis."*

- *"I'm frustrated. What can we do next?"*

After all this, there may still be no diagnosis for your child, but by being honest with your doctor, you help build a good relationship. Also remember two goals of a diagnosis: getting the services your child needs and helping that child grow. These are more important than any label.

Know How To Work With Your Health Care Team

You have a right to expect certain things when seeking health care for your child. As a first step, remember the Patient's Bill of Rights:

- *Respect for you and your child*

- *Willingness to listen patiently*

- *Taking your concerns seriously*

- *Returning phone calls promptly*

- *Courtesy from the office staff*

These are not "luxuries." Rather, they are "musts" for getting the care your child needs.

◆ Choose a doctor carefully

One of the decisions you'll face is finding a doctor for your child. People make this choice for many different reasons. Some parents choose the doctor they saw as a child. Other parents ask someone to recommend a doctor, or they seek the doctor with the best reputation. Many parents have little choice because their health plan determines which doctors their child sees.

If you have a choice of doctors, decide what skills you're looking for. Some parents value a good listener, and others want a doctor who knows the child's condition well. Ask the same question about other people who will care for your child, such as nurses and therapists.

Your child may need to see a specialist, such as a neurologist or an orthopedic surgeon. Ask your child's regular doctor to suggest a specialist. If you do not already have a regular doctor, ask parents of children with similar problems about their doctors. One way to do this is to contact a support group for your child's condition.

◆ When needed, ask for a second opinion

If you are uncertain about the diagnosis or treatment, ask for a second opinion or a referral. Many doctors feel this is a good idea. They may even welcome a second opinion.

Where do you go for a second opinion? Try a major hospital or medical center close to you. Hospitals that specialize in training doctors are another source. Ask your doctor for an idea, call your county medical society, or check with a public health agency. Your health plan may also have suggestions.

Many health plans only work with a certain group of doctors. In some cases, you may want to see a doctor who's outside that group, which means asking for a referral. Check your health plan for its policy on referrals. And whenever you choose a health plan, find out how easy it is to get a referral.

◆ When it's needed, change doctors

Some parents go to many different doctors, hoping to find one who says their child has no problem. Such "doctor shopping" often fails. A second, third, or even fourth opinion may be needed, but getting an eleventh opinion might mean parents are denying the child's problem.

There are times, however, when it's wise to try another doctor. If you feel you and the doctor simply don't understand each other or just don't get along, you may want to think about another doctor.

Chronic illness and disabilities can be hard to understand and may occasionally stump even the experts. However, if your child is not doing well and, when asked, the doctor offers no explanation, you may want to try another doctor. Some parents work with several doctors before finding the best fit for their child's needs.

Get Help In Getting The Big Picture

When caring for a child with special health needs, there are many details. The list of things you need to do is long: keeping track of medications, understanding all the treatments your child receives, finding ways to pay for health care, knowing the laws affecting services for children. Beyond these, you need to take care of yourself and other family members.

You're not alone. Many parents feel there are not enough hours in the day to get all this done. Remember that you can get help. There may be someone who can help you manage your child's care—at no extra cost. Some hospitals employ social workers (sometimes called case workers or patient counselors) for this purpose. County social service departments and public health nursing organizations can also help. Ask them about case managers for families and children.

Finding such a person is not a magic key. Case managers cannot take over your child's care. But it is useful to find extra help.

Seek out support groups. Many groups can help you meet other parents facing the same issues, who can give you more ideas on how to manage your child's care.

Get Needed Services As Soon As You Can

Some children are in danger of not getting services they may need right away in order to grow and develop, such as speech therapy, physical therapy, special education, or counseling. But it often takes time to get a service started. It may also take patience and persistence on your part.

First, you and your doctor or health professional must decide together what services are needed for your child's care. Once that is decided, find out what services are available in your community. It's best if you start this process yourself. Not all doctors know about the services and support groups that could help you. They may know about a group but have no direct experience with it. Or, doctors may feel that guiding you to services is beyond their job.

You can go directly to support groups. Ask about all the services offered for your child's condition. From there, you can get to questions about what your child needs.

Also contact public health nurses and county social workers. They should know about services available in your area.

Define Quality Care For Your Child's Condition

You are a consumer of health care. That means you're paying for a service with your money and time. Quality is important here—just like when you buy other goods or services. What things can you ask for in return? Some important points are these:

◆ Work with people who listen well and explain things clearly

Many factors go into a good relationship with your doctor, nurse, or therapist. You'll probably want someone who's open to your questions. Most parents also want someone who will explain the meaning of medical words. Many parents appreciate a person who explains things directly to the child (when the child is old enough to understand). For some children, that means using sign language or a language other than English. Beyond these, most parents want their child to be seen as another growing and learning human being. And that means seeing the person behind the illness or disability.

Decide your standards for quality care. Finding a doctor, nurse or therapist who listens well and shares information is important. When it comes to quality care, though, there's even more to think about.

Quality care means different things, depending on what parents and children want. Some examples are:

– *Working with people who know or will learn your child's medical history.*

– *Regular check-ups to preserve health and prevent problems.*

– *A health care team that gathers the facts about how your child is growing. That means complete physical exams, including other tests, such as those for hearing and vision.*

– *Detailed guidelines for daily care, medication, diet, and exercise. Depending on the child, this might also mean medical technology: inhalers for a child with asthma, blood glucose meters for children with diabetes, and the like.*

– *Short-term and long-term plans for treatment. This could range from corrective surgery to daily therapy. Plans work best when the goals and outcomes are clear and detailed.*

◆ Look for a team player

Consider finding a team player. This is a doctor who will share information about your child to other people who need it, such as classroom teachers, special education teachers, doctors, therapists, school nurses, or public health nurses. They also may be people at your insurance company or health plan, who may ask questions before deciding to pay for a service.

◆ Consider convenience

How easy is it to get to your doctor? A 15-minute drive, or an hour to a distant clinic? How's the parking? Once you're there, do you have to wait another 45 minutes, or do you see your doctor promptly? Is the clinic open when you can get there, or do you have to use your lunch hours, vacation time, and sick leave to take your child to appointments?

Being able to reach your doctor by phone can be important too. Some parents find it hard to keep explaining their child's condition to different people. They prefer talking to the same person most of the time—especially when it's an urgent call.

In some cases, you may not have much choice. Perhaps you live in a rural area without many doctors to choose from or need to see the only specialist in town who knows your child's condition.

Look at all your choices. Many parents, however, don't know the options they have. The HMO you belong to may have several locations. Or, your health plan may cover the services of another therapist close to your child's school.

◆ Different conditions call for different treatments

Each child's condition is different, and the condition may change. The treatment plan must recognize these facts.

As a first step, learn all you can about your child's condition. Some ways to do this are reading, asking questions, going to classes and workshops, and talking to other parents. A good source of help is an advocacy organization or support group. For a list of such organizations, see page 64.

◆ Clinics may be a wise choice for some conditions

For some children, a clinic is best. This is a medical group that offers a number of specialists. Here your child can see several people at one place and one time. These people can review the case as a team. Some clinics are designed to work with children with certain conditions. We are not saying that clinics are best for every child. Consider your family's needs and whether the clinic can meet them.

Prepare For Your Child's Medical Visit

Before you take your child to a medical visit, set the stage. Tell your child what to expect: why you're going, what the doctor may do, what you plan to ask about. When doing this, remember what the child knows and understands, and ask your child to express any questions or feelings. Doing so can put your child more at ease.

Often this means preparing yourself before preparing your child. Here are things to find out about and tell your child:

Note: Some of these suggestions will depend on your child's age and ability to speak and understand.

- *Who your child will see and why. Help your child understand the reason for any trip to the doctor.*
- *What tests may be uncomfortable or painful. Most parents find it best to be honest about this. Explain what the test is for, and remind the child that you'll be close by.*
- *How the child can help the appointment go well. For example, your child can answer questions and do what the doctor or nurse asks.*

For a successful visit, get your facts together. Be ready to report on your child's condition. Keep notes on how treatment is working. Note symptoms that trouble you, and any problems with daily care. List your questions and concerns ahead of time—in writing—and bring these along. Try to be specific. You can say, "Melissa only ate two meals a day for the past four days—peanut butter sandwiches and chicken soup. She also wants to go to bed at 6:30 every night." That gives your doctor more to work with than, "She doesn't eat a lot and just seems kind of tired."

Know How To Talk With Your Health Care Team

If you have questions listed ahead of time, you've already laid the groundwork. Try a "dry run" before seeing the doctor. Practice asking your questions to your spouse or a friend.

Most doctors, nurses, and therapists welcome questions. This is the only way they can speak to your concerns. Keep asking questions until you get answers—even when you have to repeat yourself. If something confuses you, say so. You have a right to understand your child's care.

Observe your child's behavior closely, and write down what you see in a notebook or journal. Ask about any behaviors that you don't understand.

Perhaps you feel frustrated when there's not enough time to discuss problems or raise questions during a regular office visit. If so, ask if you can schedule a special appointment to ask questions. Find out if you'll be charged for this and how much. If there is a charge, ask if your health plan will pay it.

Avoid Self-Defeating Ideas

Certain feelings make it hard for parents to talk to people on the health care team. You may not even be aware of these feelings. Let's look at some now:

◆ **"Put your child in the doctor's hands"**

This idea may sound comforting. But it's not really a good idea. After all, you are a partner in your child's care. What you think, feel, and do about your child's health care matters a lot, so do your child's feelings and actions.

◆ **"There's a perfect doctor for my child somewhere"**

We urge you to find a doctor who listens to your concerns and treats you and your child with respect. Yet doctors are only human. The problems presented by your child's condition may be frustrating to the doctor as well as to you. There may not be a ready answer to some questions.

◆ **"This approach will finally solve the problem"**

It helps to know about new treatments and procedures. It's important, however, to remember that most chronic health conditions will not be "cured" or "solved;" they may only be improved or relieved.

Keep Your Own Records

It's a good idea to keep track of important procedures, changes in your child's behavior, dates of important tests, and the like. Remember that children with special health needs sometimes have thick files at the doctor's office. Finding anything in that file may take some time.

Think about buying a spiral or loose leaf notebook to keep your own records. But before you do this, consider two things.

First, ask what information is worth saving and what's not. You don't want a file cabinet full of unused information that sits in the corner. Try keeping records for a while and see what you actually go back and refer to. If you never refer to a file, throw it out.

Also, don't feel you have to keep a lot of records—or many records at all. Do what's best for you. Some people find that having detailed records makes them feel "on top of things." Others don't like storing a lot of paper. For them, keeping a small loose leaf notebook for current questions may be enough. Older information can just be filed away.

If you do keep records, the following are some things to note:

- *The dates, nature, and results of all tests or surgery.*
- *Comments from your doctor, specialist, or therapist.*
- *Results from any conference, evaluation, or progress report on your child.*
- *All medications your child currently takes. Include the names, dates, doses, times, and results you observe.*
- *Allergies to food or medication.*
- *Any change in your child's condition.*
- *Programs and schools your child attends. Include the names of teachers or therapists and the dates of attendance.*
- *Contagious diseases your child has had, such as chicken pox and measles.*
- *Advice from anyone who provides services for your child, such as therapists and teachers.*
- *A list of all people who've provided care for your child. Include the person's name, type of service, and each person's role, along with the date. Note where each service took place.*
- *Money matters: Contracts with your health plan, bills for medical services, and insurance payments. Also include information on other programs that help you pay for health care, such as Medicaid or Social Security.*
- *Immunizations (shots) your child has received. These can get overlooked when a child has a chronic health condition.*

– Milestones in your child's growth. Note first words, first tries at walking, and any other accomplishments.

Take notes on what the doctor, nurse, or therapist says. Doing so will help you remember the details when you have to explain them to someone else, such as your child's teacher. Writing helps you put the facts in your own words and get things clear in your own mind. Doing so may reduce stress as well.

There are many ways to take notes, so pick a system that works for you. Some parents ask for copies of any notes that doctors or nurses make, or your clinic might be willing to send a letter that sums up the information.

Do you have access to a personal computer? If you do, then consider keeping your records on the computer. When shopping for a computer, explain to the sales person how you plan to use it and ask for advice about what to buy.

Give Medical Information To Everyone Who Needs It

Your child's school, camp, or day care need to know about any chronic illness or disability. Check to make sure they have the right information on your child. Also see that your child's records are transferred if you move, change schools, or change doctors. Transferring records can take up to one month, so plan ahead. If you keep extra copies of records, ask if you can send those to cut down on the time required.

CHAPTER 2 / Learning
How To Be
Assertive

When it comes to services for your child, think of this saying: "Persistence pays." It can take time and patience to get needed services. That's when you need to advocate for your child. Advocating means getting what's rightfully yours, and that may take being assertive.

Some parents have the wrong idea about assertiveness. Too often people take this word to mean "angry," "aggressive," or "offensive." This is not true.

The Coordinating Council for Handicapped Children, a group in Chicago, trains parents to be assertive. In *How to Get Services by Being Assertive,* this group lists several ways to complete the sentence "Assertiveness is..." Some examples:

- *expressing your needs clearly and directly.*

- *expressing your ideas without feeling guilty.*

- *sticking up for what you think your child needs—even though the "experts" may not agree.*

Under "Assertiveness is not...," they list statements such as:

- *beating around the bush before stating your needs.*

- *feeling too guilty or afraid to express your needs.*
- *agreeing with professionals—no matter how you feel— because "professionals know what is best."*

In all of this, don't assume professionals (nurses, doctors, therapists, insurance companies) are the "bad guys." Assertiveness does not mean assuming the worst of people. In many cases, these people may feel trapped by a rigid system, too. They may be victims of red tape or funding cuts. Professionals can feel the same fear and frustration you do.

Developing Assertiveness Skills

Assertiveness is like learning to drive: It's a skill you learn and practice over time. What makes up that skill? These are some answers:

◆ Disagree without being disagreeable

You want the best health care for your child. That's the real goal—not scoring points, making people feel guilty, or dividing the world into "Us" and "Them." In fact, the way to assert your power is to be calm, well-informed, prepared, and persistent. Remember your goals and stick to one issue at a time.

If you're angry, it's best to control that feeling during a meeting. Later, when you're with a friend, you can blow off steam.

◆ Remember that meetings or medical visits are not a social time

Being assertive may mean disagreeing or asking a hard question. That's OK. Politeness and "niceness" are not the main points at a medical visit. These visits are for people to solve problems and get information. While it's good to agree and build good relationships, the major purpose is to get good care.

At times it helps to bring along a friend or someone else who can support you. Some parents even like to "rehearse" before a difficult meeting. This means asking a friend to "play the part" of the doctor or other professional, giving you a chance to practice asking your questions before the meeting.

◆ Express your own feelings without blaming others

The trick here is to put across more "I" messages than "You" messages. What do we mean? Look at the following pair of statements:

– *"You're the doctor. You're the expert on my child's condition. Why aren't you doing more to help us?"*

– *"I'm learning everything I can about my child's condition. We want to do everything we can to manage it well. What do you suggest we do?"*

The first statement is a "You" message and the second is an "I" message. "You" messages place the blame on others. They give the impression that you, as a parent, are not in control but are at the mercy of others.

"I" messages are different. They make it clear that you're in charge of your feelings, and that you'll take any action needed. These are true assertive statements.

◆ Work at understanding

Understanding another person is a two-way process. You can't control how well another person will listen, but you can make sure you're doing your part.

What does this mean? We recommend:

– *taking careful notes at all meetings*

– *writing follow-up letters that list the decisions made at the meeting*

– *asking your health plan to confirm a decision—in writing*

– *listing your questions before a meeting and setting an agenda*

– *doing your homework and building your case.*

In short, it means taking action and being prepared.

◆ Set time limits

For example, your HMO promises to refer you to a specialist in two weeks. The date goes by and nothing happens. You have a right to bring this up. Or if your insurance company agrees to pay for speech therapy within 30 days, you can justifiably expect them to send a check in that time.

In cases like these, make it clear you'll follow up if a date is missed. If the appointment is delayed, the meeting is postponed, or the service isn't paid for, say something.

◆ Learn the jargon

The professionals you work with may use a lot of terms that are new to you. People in health care, insurance, education, and social services may all have their own "jargon."

While hearing all these new words, you may feel like a visitor in a foreign country who doesn't speak the language. Take heart, the feeling is normal.

Always ask for answers in terms you can understand. Also, learn as many of the new words as you can. For a start, see the Glossary on page 72 and the materials listed under For Further Reading on page 61.

◆ **Get training**

Several agencies offer training for parents of children with a chronic illness or disability. Take advantage of them. Contact the Federation For Children With Special Needs at 312 Stuart Street, Boston, MA 02116, (617) 482-2915 for a referral to an agency in your area that might offer this service

◆ **Set reasonable goals**

Start with one small issue and try to be assertive. This can build your confidence and help you tackle larger problems.

◆ **Be willing to compromise**

Agreeing on part of an issue is often a start in the right direction. You may be able to work on the rest of an issue after completing the first step.

CHAPTER 3 / Handling The Emotional Impact Of Your Child's Condition

Raising a child with special health needs takes a lot of skill. It often seems you have to do a lot of "head work": writing letters, making calls, keeping bills straight. But "tending to the heart" is just as important. You want to love and care for your child. That means caring for yourself too.

Chances are good that you'll feel many things, sometimes all at once. Those feelings may seem to go against each other: love for your child, and pain over your situation; hope for a better treatment, and despair when nothing seems to improve; feeling strong enough to handle any situation, and giving up hope.

All parents who manages their child's health care experience stress. It can be a big job, so give yourself permission not to do it perfectly. It's healthy to realize that there are limits to what you can do. The important thing is not to deny your feelings or feel guilty about them. Any feeling is okay. Just let them come to the surface and work through them.

Talk to your spouse, partner, family members, close friends, or anyone else you trust. You can also try church groups. Seek out other parents, especially those whose children have chronic conditions. A parent who's "been there" and knows what it's like is often the best support in the world.

Self-help groups and disability organizations offer parent support. Many have formal programs on caring for children with a chronic illness or disability. Through them, you'll get a chance to meet other parents facing the same issues.

See a counselor if you feel the need. This can really help if you've felt depressed or overwhelmed for days or weeks at a time. Again, your support group or hospital can make suggestions.

Get Help With Daily Tasks

You don't have to do it all alone. Besides offering emotional support, other people can help with daily tasks, including household chores and daily care for your child. Professional caregivers or home health aides can help. Some health plans and public programs will pay for all or part of these services.

You can also look for informal help. Many people may be willing to care for your child if you'll let them. Talk to family, friends, and church groups, or consider hiring a neighbor to care for your child an hour each day.

Find Support For Your Child

We've mentioned several times that you can get support from other parents. Children also need the support of peers. Seek out support groups for your child. Doing so can help your child build self-esteem and make it through worry, fear, and just feeling "down."

Many options exist for children with specific conditions. For example, there are summer camps for children with diabetes, asthma, seizure disorders, and other chronic illnesses. Some school districts and cities offer social and sports events for children with special needs. Remember that your child can also get emotional support from children without disabilities or chronic illness.

Find Respite Care

All of us need time for ourselves, but setting aside such time can be harder if your child has special health needs. That's why you may need to plan special "time off." This time is called respite care or short-term care.

This doesn't have to be a formal program. You can get informal respite care from family, friends, or church groups. However, formal respite care is available. For instance, your county social service agency may offer respite care. Summer camps for children with disabilities can give you needed respite, and provide a good experience for your child. You might also find volunteers to care for your child for several hours a week while you take care of other duties.

It is important to get respite care for even a short time when you can. When relatives, church members or friends ask what they can do for you, ask them for respite care. Teaching them to do your child's daily care will allow you to have some time for yourself. If your child's care requires special training, a public health nurse may be able to provide it. Such small gifts to yourself and your family members can add up.

Some final notes: You don't have to find respite care. In fact, you may feel that you have enough time to yourself already. Perhaps family and friends provide enough help with your child's care. But if you do use respite care, don't feel guilty about it. You're simply giving yourself time that any parent needs. Respite care does not mean you feel your child is a burden, nor does it shows a lack of love for the child. Taking the time for yourself can help you regain energy and feel more loving to your family. That's one of the best things you do for your child.

PART 2 / Paying
For
Your
Child's
Care

CHAPTER 4 / Getting Started

When your child has a disability or chronic illness, paying for health care can be a daily concern. That's the reason for this section of the book. Our aim is to help you pay for your child's health care, which means knowing your options. It also means knowing which programs are right for you, finding them, and making them work together.

For many of us, the first step is health insurance. This area may be confusing at first. However, following certain guidelines can help. In addition, insurance is not your only option and may be just one part of a total "system" that pays for your child's care. In Chapter 5 you'll find more details on the different kinds of health plans and public programs offered today. Knowing about them can help you decide what kind of plan is best for your child. Chapter 6 offers ideas that have helped many parents come to grips with health plans.

There may be times when you disagree with your health plan about what services should be covered. Chapter 7 will offer advice on how to best handle these situations.

As you read, we hope you find tools that really work. There's a lot of information here, but don't let that concern you. Take only the ideas that apply to your family and act on just one or two ideas at a time. Break the ideas down into small tasks; small enough that you can do them right away. For example, one suggestion is to understand what services your health insurance pays for. If that sounds like a big job, divide it into smaller jobs:

1. *Find your copy of the policy*

2. *Set aside one hour to start reading the policy*

3. *List your questions about the policy*

4. *Make a list of people who can answer your questions*

5. *Get phone numbers for those people*

Above all, keep looking for options. Knowing what your options are can help you provide the best care for your child—and meet the medical bills.

Options For Uninsured Families

If you are one of the millions of American families without some form of health coverage, there are still ways you may find assistance in paying for quality health care for your child.

In Part 4, we have listed some programs and options you may want to explore. As with any new project you start, take your time and follow through. Don't get frustrated or discouraged if your questions aren't answered right away. Keep contacting agencies listed in Part 4 until you have a clear picture of what options are available for you and your child.

CHAPTER 5 / Types Of
Health Plans
Offered
Today

There are a variety of insurance plans and options. It is important to understand the different types of plans available, either through your employer or on your own. The following pages discuss the different plans you'll want to know about.

Traditional Fee-For-Service Plans

Fee-for-service plans are sold by many companies, including Allstate, Prudential, State Farm, and Aetna. Blue Cross & Blue Shield also sell this type of plan. They're called "traditional" policies because for many years they were the only kind of health plans sold.

Today, you may have other options, such as health maintenance organizations (HMOs) and preferred provider organizations (PPOs). We'll describe these options later in this chapter.

29

Traditional policies are all different. Still, many have these features:

◆ **The doctor gets paid for the services your policy covers**

This kind of insurance is also called "fee-for-service" coverage. With some policies, you may need to pay for the service and the insurance company will reimburse you. With other policies, the insurance company gets the bill.

◆ **Often you can choose the doctors and hospitals you'll use**

In fact, your range of choice is usually greater with this kind of plan than with HMOs or PPOs. However, this is not always true. Some traditional policies may restrict your choices.

◆ **You'll have to pay some costs out of your pocket—besides the premium**

Often these include copayments, deductibles, and bills for services the plan does not cover. Such costs can add up fast.

◆ **Often the plan covers only basic care—care that is "medically necessary"**

What does "medically necessary" mean? This differs from plan to plan. Often it means care for an "acute" condition—one that last only for a short time. Such a plan may not cover preventive care: routine physicals, hearing aids, or custodial care.

The policy will list the services it covers. However, some services are not covered at all. You'll often see these listed in a section called "Exclusions" or "Limitations." Read these carefully. Never assume that a service your child needs is covered.

◆ **Differences between group and individual coverage**

Many organizations offer group plans to their members or employees. Examples are businesses, credit unions, and labor unions. Often group plans have certain advantages, such as lower cost. The company can spread the costs and risks among a group of people. As a result, you'll pay a lower premium than if you were buying the coverage elsewhere. Other benefits are broader coverage and lower copayments. Individual coverage is when you buy health benefits for one person. The benefit contract is designed for the person's needs. This coverage is often much more expensive and difficult to get than group coverage.

Besides this, many group plans offer "open enroll-ment" periods. During these periods you can sign up for a health plan, and you won't have to fill out a health history. That means you don't have to describe any conditions that might cause an insurer to turn you or your family members down for coverage.

◆ **Add up all the costs**

Copayments, deductibles, premiums, and exclusions are words that mean bills for you to pay. When you look at any traditional insurance policy, be sure to estimate all these possible costs and add them up.

Health Maintenance Organizations (HMOs)

HMOs offer a wide range of medical services for a fixed premium. This kind of coverage is also called a "prepaid" plan. That means the monthly premium pays for all covered services in advance.

◆ **Comparing HMOs and traditional insurance. How are HMOs different from traditional insurance?**

- *With an HMO, you or your employer pay the monthly premium. Beyond that, many HMO members never see a medical bill. The premium covers all covered services you use during the month. There's no separate fee for each service. However, you may have to pay reduced fees for some services. Examples are fees for eyeglasses or medicine.*

- *The HMO is often a medical clinic and an insurance company rolled into one. In other words, the HMO may handle your medical coverage and your medical care. (With some HMOs, this is not true.)*

- *Most of the time, you can only see the doctors who are part of the HMO. However, that list of doctors may be large. The doctor you want to see may already be on the list, or the HMO might refer you to that doctor.*

- *HMOs include some preventive care in the monthly premium. You pay little or nothing for these services. However, an HMO may not pay for certain services a child with chronic illness or disability needs: occupa-tional therapy, speech therapy, hearing aids, and the like. The HMO may not consider these to be preventive care.*

- *The specialist your child needs to see may not be one of the HMO's doctors. Sometimes, though, the HMO will refer you to this person. After the first referral, the HMO may even let you contact the specialist directly.*

Again, do not assume anything. Get a written statement on referrals from the HMO. Ask these questions: How is a referral done? How long does it take? Will the HMO pay for the referral? Are there any exceptions to what's written in the policy?

Keep in mind that HMOs are all different, and so are their benefits and premiums. Some plans combine features of HMOs and traditional insurance. For example, one plan offers HMO coverage when you see certain doctors. If you see other doctors, you get traditional coverage. Plans designed this way are called combination plans.

◆ Costs to you

Even if you belong to an HMO, you may still have to pay some fees beyond a monthly premium. Your policy, for example, may only cover 80 percent of the cost for mental health treatments. Other services may not be covered at all. You may also have to pay for prescription drugs, though these fees may be greatly reduced.

◆ Differences between group and individual coverage

As with traditional insurance, many HMOs offer both group and individual memberships. Generally, the two advantages of group membership we mentioned earlier also apply to HMOs: lower premiums than individual policies, and open enrollment periods. Not all HMOs offer individual memberships and others even limit the number of individual members. If you apply for an individual membership, you may have to fill out a detailed medical history. The HMO may deny you if you or a family member already has a chronic illness or disability.

◆ Advantages and disadvantages of HMOs for children with special health needs

An HMO may have advantages for children with chronic conditions. But you may also find disadvantages:

- *Treatment is provided only by staff doctors. These may not include specialists in rare disabilities. Also, clinics for certain disabilities may not be included.*
- *There may be no HMOs nearby. This is especially true in rural areas with only a few clinics or hospitals.*

Preferred Provider Organizations (PPOs)

Some people think of Preferred Provider Organizations (PPOs) as HMOs; however, PPOs are different. These are the basic ideas behind PPOs:

- *An insurance company or self-insured employer contracts with a limited group of doctors and hospitals.*
- *These doctors and hospitals lower their fees for members of the PPO. In return, the providers and hospitals see more patients.*

Many of the points we made about HMOs and fee-for service insurance also apply to PPOs. As always, decide if the PPO's coverage meets your family's needs.

Self-Insured Plans

Your employer may offer several options for health plans. In fact, most large companies provide a "menu" of choices. Those choices may include HMOs, traditional plans, and PPOs.

However, some companies have another way to provide health plans. Instead of paying an outside insurer, a company may set up its own fund to pay for the plan. In other words, the company insures itself.

With a self-insured company, the money to pay for health care usually comes from the company's cash flow. Or, it may come from a trust fund the company sets up. Small companies who want to self insure work with other companies to set up a joint trust fund. Sometimes a self-insured company buys insurance to cover large medical costs.

When comparing health plans, note that some self-insured plans are handled by an outside group. Why should this matter to you? For three reasons.

First, a self-insured plan may look just like an HMO or private insurance plan. This is especially true when the self-insured plan is managed by an outside insurance company.

Second, you can't assume you'll get the same benefits from a self-insured plan as from an HMO or other private insurer. Many states require other private insurers to provide certain kinds of benefits. However, large self-insured plans are not controlled by state law and do not have to provide mandated benefits. (Mandated benefits are certain benefits required by state law.)

If you enroll in a large self-insured plan, you might receive mandated benefits anyway. However, many smaller firms cannot afford them and often don't offer mandated benefits.

Third, self-insured plans are controlled differently than other plans. At some point you may disagree with your health insurer about which medical costs they should pay and which costs you have to pay. This might happen, for example, when the company denies a payment for one of your child's medical bills. You may decide to appeal this decision and file a complaint.

If you belong to an HMO, you can file the complaint with the state agency that regulates HMOs. Or if you belong to a fee-for-service plan, you can go to the state commissioner's office. With a self-insured plan, however, filing a complaint is harder since these plans are not controlled by state law. The complaint filing process is decided by the employer. You may want to find out how to use this "appeal" process before making a decision on an insurance plan.

A Note About Private Plans

Fee-for-service insurance, HMOs, PPOs, and self-insured companies are often called "private" plans. This sets them apart from public plans such as Medicaid and Medicare. However, public and private health plans are becoming more alike. They offer similar benefits and try to contain costs in similar ways.

Public Programs

Certain health plans are funded by the federal government, state government, or a pool of funds from private insurers. We call these health plans "public plans." The public plans to know about are listed in the following section.

◆ **Medicaid**

You might also hear this plan called "Medical Assistance," "MA," or "Title 19." All these names refer to the same program.

Medicaid is a program funded jointly by the state and federal government, which provides free medical care to low income persons. It also provides health care to people who receive Aid to Families with Dependent Children (AFDC). If you are eligible for Supplemental Security Income (SSI), you are eligible for Medicaid in most states. People receiving SSI must apply for Medicaid. Families who receive Medicaid because of AFDC or SSI eligibility are called *categorically eligible*.

If you take part in Medicaid, you'll receive an eligibility card. The state sends this card to you each month that you are eligible for the program. When receiving health care, drugs, or medical supplies, you must present this card to the provider. That provider must be enrolled to take part in Medicaid. The doctor then sends a bill to the Medicaid program.

You may be able to qualify for Medicaid even if your income is too high for SSI or AFDC. This is true if you are classified as medically needy. Families in this group usually have large medical bills that reduce their income. Taking those bills into account is called a *spend down*. States having a medically needy program must make coverage available to pregnant women and children who would be categorically needy but for income. Many medically needy programs cover additional categories. Check in your state to see if your child is eligible. After the spend down, the family may qualify for Medicaid.

As of July 1, 1990, parents of children with disabilities who are Medicaid eligible without taking into account parental income will be expected to contribute a fee based on family need. This is called the *parental fee contribution* and is based on income exceeding 200% of federal poverty guidelines.

State Medicaid programs are mandated by federal law to cover certain services. These services include:

- *inpatient hospital services*
- *outpatient hospital services*
- *rural health clinic services*
- *lab and x-ray services*
- *skilled nursing facility services*
- *health services for individuals 21 years of age or older*
- *physician services*
- *family planning services*
- *nurse-midwife services*

- *early and periodic screening and diagnosis and treatment services (EPSDT) for individuals under 21 years of age*

State Medicaid programs have the option of covering additional services, known as optional services. Inclusion of optional services in the state Medicaid plan is determined according to the availability of dollars within an individual state.

The states may impose limitations on the services they pay for under the Medicaid program. States may specifically limit the amount, scope and duration of services of mandatory and optional services. For example, some states limit the number of inpatient hospital days over a designated period of time that will be reimbursed.

States generally must make covered services available to all Medicaid beneficiaries within a categorial group. This requirement is known as the "comparability" requirement. States generally also must make the same service coverage available throughout the state. This requirement is known as the "statewideness" requirement.

There are limits to some services. Other services beyond certain limits may need to be authorized first. Your doctor, nurse, or therapist should take care of the authorization.

If you take part in Medicaid, you'll have to do certain things. For one, you must report changes in your income, savings, family size, property ownership, address, or health insurance. You must also report lawsuits or legal action to collect money for accidents or injuries.

Once or twice per year, the state reviews families on Medicaid to see if they're still eligible for the program. This requires filling out certain forms. It also means sending in other papers such as bank statements.

To find out more about Medicaid, write or call your county social service agency.

◆ **Medicare**

Medicare is a health insurance program from the federal government. It covers many medical services, including hospital care, doctor care, and care from a skilled nursing facility.

Medicare applies to people over age 65 and to certain people with disabilities. Those people with disabilities include adult children of parents receiving Social Security benefits.

People in end-stage renal dialysis are also included. Individuals who have chronic kidney disease can get dialysis and transplants under Medicare at any age.

Medicare may require you to pay deductibles. You may also have to pay part of the bill for certain covered services. This percentage is called a copayment and can be as high as 20 percent.

Note that Medicare and Medicaid are different programs, even though they have similar names. To find out more about Medicare, contact your local Social Security office. When you do, you can ask for two booklets: "Your Medicare Handbook" and "Medicare Coverage for Kidney Dialysis and Kidney Transplant Services."

State High Risk Pools

State high risk health insurance pools are available in many states. These pools are established to provide health insurance coverage to individuals and families who cannot get health insurance coverage because of existing health problems.

The pools vary in each state they are offered, but usually require that families pay premiums like they would for traditional insurance plans. They may also have deductibles and copays for services, similar to other health care payment options.

To find out whether your state has a high risk pool, call your state insurance commissioner. Be sure to get information on eligibility criteria and the cost of participating in the pool.

CHAPTER 6 / Coming To Terms With Health Plans

The health care expenses related to a child with a disability or chronic illness can be a challenge for you. It can also be a challenge for your employer or the company that helps pay your medical bills. It is important to keep in mind your responsibility as a consumer. Public programs and private insurers have large demands for services from a great many people. By being a responsible consumer and using only the services you or your child needs and at the level of your need, will help to keep insurance premiums and taxes from continually rising.

Every child and family is different. That means the services and insurance your child requires are unique. So, you expect that getting the health plan your child needs may take planning, energy, time, and extra expense.

Consider some of these issues parents have faced:

◆ Getting insurance coverage

Some private insurers may change the policy to exclude a child with special health care needs, or may cover the child at first and then drop the coverage later.

◆ Paying for health insurance

When considering health plans for their children, many parents simply look at the monthly premium. The actual costs may be higher, however. Deductibles, copayments, and payments for services not covered by your health plan can add to your bills.

Note: If you're not familiar with words such as "deductibles" and "copayments," you can look them up in the Glossary on page 72.

We'll also explain them in this section of the book.

◆ Getting coverage for all the services needed

As an example, a public health nurse feels that a child needs speech therapy. The parents assume that their insurance pays for this expense. Later they read the policy and face a surprise. Speech therapy is not covered. This is the kind of surprise you want to avoid.

◆ Disagreeing with your insurer about what should be covered

For example, a child needs a motorized wheelchair. His parents ask the doctor to order one, and they assume their insurance company will pay the bill for $4,650. However, the insurance company denies the claim, saying the wheelchair is not "medically necessary." They also say the cost goes above "usual and customary charges." The parents disagree, but they don't know what to do.

We don't mean to sound negative. Many insurers cooperate fully in caring for children with special health needs. Some families pay the extra costs with no financial burden.

Keep in mind, however, your medical bills may rise each year. This means you may need to be creative. Instead of relying on one source to cover your medical bills, you may have to combine several. Families with two working parents may have two different health plans. Knowing your options helps, and that's the purpose of this section.

One note about the word "insurance." Payment for medical bills comes from many different sources. Some are insurance companies. Others include health maintenance organizations (HMOs), Preferred Provider Organizations (PPOs), and Blue Cross/Blue Shield. Federal, state, and local government is also part of the picture. Some employers don't use any of these sources. Instead they "self-insure"—pay for their own health benefits. Chapter 5 describes these types of health plans.

Not all of these sources offer insurance in the usual meaning of that word. To keep things simpler, we use the words "health plan" or "insurance" to mean any source of funds that help pay for health care. Your "insurer" is any company or agency that helps you pay medical bills. Also, the words "policy" and "plan" mean any contract that spells out what your health benefits are.

Asking Questions About Your Health Plan

Insurance plans can be hard to read. Even when you ask questions about a plan, the answers may be confusing, or the insurer may not know how their coverage applies to your child.

There are two good reasons to know about health plans, however. Obviously, you want the best possible care for your child. Second, you don't want any surprises about what services your plan will pay for. Surprises could mean extra bills for you to pay. You don't want to find out at the last minute that the surgery your child needs is not covered. Nor do you want to pay half the fees for the physical therapist, when you thought your plan would pay all of them.

Fortunately, there are ways to answer questions about health plans. Some of the things you can do are:

◆ **Learn about health plans**

You can start learning about health plans from this book. We'll also suggest ways to find out more.

If health plans are explained clearly, you can learn what you need to know. You don't need to be an expert. You only need to know whether your insurance will meet your family's needs.

◆ **Learn about yourself**

You can learn to recognize the feelings that make it hard to learn about health plans. Often just labelling a feeling—

"There's that old fear of money matters again"—can go a long way to getting rid of it.

◆ **Get support**

Remember that other parents have learned to feel confident about paying for health care. Join a parents' group or support group for your child's condition to hear other people's stories and hopefully learn from their experiences.

◆ **Rely on yourself**

You don't have to depend on hearsay to learn about health plans. You can do better than getting over-the-fence advice from your next-door neighbor. You often get the best information by looking into the facts yourself.

◆ **Gain confidence**

Remember that you're doing a major job already by raising a child with special health care needs. You're the person who sees the whole picture. If your child is a minor, you probably keep track of all the health care, which makes you an expert along with your child's doctor. Knowing this can help you feel more confident.

In the following pages, we'll explain how to get started in these areas.

Know Your Coverage

◆ **Read the contract**

If you already have a health plan, the first step is to read the policy or contract carefully. You'll probably run across things you don't understand. That's OK, so don't let it stop you. Just write down your questions on a separate sheet of paper and keep on reading.

◆ **Get answers**

Next, ask questions, and keep asking until you understand the answers. Your main sources of answers are materials and people.

In addition to this book, good sources of information are any brochures, booklets, or manuals about your health plan. For other sources of information, see "For Further Reading" on page 61.

People you can turn to for answers to your questions include:

- **Your employer.** *If you have group coverage, start with your personnel, employee benefits, or group insurance department. Explain that you have questions about your child's health care and need to talk with someone.*

- **Your insurance agent.** *If you bought health insurance through an agent, go to that person with your questions. If your employer is self-insured, find out who administers the plan and who can answer questions. It helps to always work with the same person.*

- **Your doctor, nurse, or therapist.** *These people may know about health plans—especially about how they affect your child's care.*

- **Someone from your health plan.** *The person you need to contact may have one of many titles: patient representative, consumer representative, benefits coordinator, customer service representative, policy- holder service representative, or patient counselor. Keep track of the name of the person who was able to help you with your question. It helps to work with the same person each time.*

- **Your support group.** *Throughout this book, we mention the option of joining a group of people who share your concerns. This group could be a parents group or an organization that works just with your child's condition. Besides giving you more information, these groups can provide emotional support. For a list of such groups see page 64.*

When you ask these people questions, get the important answers in writing.

◆ As you research your plan, look for key words

No matter what health plan you have, look for certain words:

- *Who are the* **insureds***?*

  That is, who are the people covered under the plan?

- *What are the* **deductibles***?*

  These are payments you'll have to make out of your own pocket before your insurance will apply.

- ***What are the exclusions?***

  These are things the policy does not cover. Read these carefully to see if any service, medications, or equip ment your child needs is excluded. This section may have another title, such as "Limitations" or "What's Not Covered."

- *Is there a **pre-existing condition** clause?*

These deny coverage for a condition that starts before the policy began. They may also deny coverage for an adopted child with a chronic health condition. Or, the policy may cover such conditions—but only after a waiting period. Those waiting periods can vary from six months to several years. A pre-existing condition may also limit coverage under the policy.

- *Is there a **cancellation** or **non-renewal** provision?*

That is, when can the insurer cancel the plan? Can the plan be cancelled for one or more family members?

- *Is there a **maximum liability** on the policy?*

Most insurance policies have a maximum liability clause that establishes the total amount the insurer will pay in claims over the insured's lifetime. These lifetime maximums vary widely from policy to policy. Policies sometimes set a total amount the insurer will pay for claims in connection with a specific kind of health problem. Policies may also have annual ceilings, which state a maximum amount of coverage for a 12 month period.

- *How about **continuation** rights?*

This applies when you receive group health insurance through an employer. The term refers to options to continue health insurance:

– *For yourself if you become disabled or leave your job.*

– *For your child when he or she reaches a certain age.*

Federal law says that an insurer must continue your policy if you're covered under a group plan and become disabled or lose your job. However, you may have to pay the full premium for the group plan. This premium may be several times what you pay now.

Likewise, some states have laws that require that coverage continue for children as they become adults. In the past, insurers could end coverage when a child reached a certain age or finished college. Today the insurer must continue the coverage if the child cannot work and still depends on you for support.

To continue coverage, you may have to furnish proof of your child's age. The insurer may also require this proof at future dates. This means filling out a form the company will send you.

- *What are your **conversion** options?*

That is, how do you convert from a group policy to an individual policy?

This question is important because it's often easier for you to get group insurance than individual insurance. This is often true when your child has a chronic illness or disability. Group coverage is also usually less expensive.

What happens to your health plan if your employer cancels the group policy? When this happened in the past, it was hard for a child with special health needs to get new health insurance. Now most states have laws requiring the insurer to give you a choice: You can convert your group policy to an individual policy. In this case, you don't have to meet any new requirements (provide *evidence of insurability*) to get the individual policy. The new policy, however, does not have to include all benefits that were provided under the group plan and the premium will be higher.

- *What about **coordination of benefits**?*

This applies when you and your spouse both receive health plans through your jobs. In that case, one plan becomes "primary." The primary plan is the first to pay covered costs. The second plan picks up covered costs not paid by the primary plan.

- *Is there a **grace period** for paying premiums?*

Some plans allow payment up to 30 days after the premium is due.

◆ **Be aware of benefits mandated by state law**

As mentioned earlier, many states have laws requiring health insurers to offer certain benefits. Among the services that have been mandated under state laws are home health care, mental health services and chemical dependency treatment. Self-insured companies do not have to provide mandated benefits. If you feel your policy does not offer a mandated benefit, ask about this right away.

44

Mastering Health Plans: Some General Guidelines

Each child and health plan is unique. In this book, we can only give general guidelines on choosing health plans. Much of what follows is information to help you make that choice. We realize that you may have no choice. For example, some employers have cut back on health benefits to control costs. Others have made employees share more of the cost of their plans. Some parents change jobs and go to a new employer who offers fewer benefits. Parents who are self-employed will also have limited options.

When it comes to choosing health plans, the following are some pointers used by parents we know:

- *Start by thinking about your family's needs. First, determine your child's current and long-term needs. Then compare the plans open to you.*

    For example, some children need coverage for surgical care or mental health care. Others need coverage for home health care or a private nurse. Still other children need to rent or buy medical equipment, e.g., wheel chairs, prostheses, braces. Some plans may offer better coverage for these different needs.

- *When comparing plans, you may find that they all begin to sound alike. There's a reason for this: Many kinds of health plans now control costs in similar ways.*

    So, if you're choosing a health plan, look for ways they differ. Look especially for the **key words** mentioned earlier in this chapter under "Know Your Coverage," page 42, (e.g., insureds, deductibles, copayments, exclusions). These words can make a big difference in your child's care.

- *Remember that there's no such thing as a "standard" plan. Although plans offer some similar benefits, each plan is different. Find out exactly what your plan covers.*

- *When looking at health plans, you'll compare printed materials. These include brochures, plan summaries, and the like. It's good to read these materials, but remember many of these are general. They are not the actual contract. **Only the policy or contract is legally binding**.*

- *Verify your coverage by **getting it in writing**. For example, you may count on your plan to pay 100 percent of your child's physical therapy fees. If so, make sure the*

45

plan says this. If you're not sure it does, then find out what the plan **does** pay. Write to your employee benefits department and ask them to confirm your coverage in writing—in words you understand.

- Look for any "riders" or "endorsements" to your plan, which change or limit the basic coverage. Finding one in your policy should raise a red flag: It means your plan has been changed.

Some plans simply include a rider that denies coverage for certain long-term illnesses or disabilities. This could increase your out-of-pocket costs. Riders could also make it hard to get the services your child needs. It is best to find out exactly how the rider will affect your child. If your child's needs are not fully covered, consider another source of funds.

- Understand that some plans limit your choice of doctors and hospitals. For example, HMOs and PPOs contract only with certain doctors and hospitals. If your child receives care from one of these people, the coverage applies. But if you go to a doctor who's not on the "official list," you will have to pay for it.

You might feel it's important to keep working with your child's current doctor. Then ask that person: If we choose this plan, will we still be able to see you? Once you've got the answer, decide what you can live with.

- Look at the deductible. A plan with lower deductibles— $50, $100, $200—will cost you more in the long run than a policy with a deductible of $1,000. The policy with the higher deductible will cover the most expensive and long-term costs. It's those costs that can drain family finances—not the $1,000 deductible.

- Consider what would happen to your child's health care if you change jobs. Before you make the change, find out what the health benefits will be for your child. You may even want to contact the company offering those benefits. After you take these facts into account, you may decide not to change jobs.

- Also consider how your health plan will change if you lose your job or divorce. Some states have laws requiring that insurance for dependent children continue after the divorce becomes final. Be sure to talk about this with your lawyer.

If you lose your job, federal law allows you to continue any group coverage you received. However, you will have to pay the full cost for this coverage. Your employer is required to explain these options to you within 10 days after you leave the company. Even so, you might want to research this now.

- *Health plans are not set in stone. Some companies are willing to change the written contract—especially when it saves money. This may also result in better care for your child. For example, your health plan might agree to pay for home care rather than care in a hospital. So ask questions. Find out how flexible your plan is willing to be.*

If you decide to do this, you'll need to tell your employer or your health plan about your child's needs. Some parents don't like to do this. They fear their child's health benefits will be cut back if someone finds out how much care the child needs. This can be a hard decision. Keeping one thing in mind may help: To get answers to your questions, you'll have to talk about what care your child really needs. Think about how much information you'll need to provide in doing that.

Think, too, about the person you'll talk to. Often this is someone from your employee benefits department. Perhaps you won't feel at ease talking with this person. In that case, consider going directly to someone at your health plan.

Suppose you think of a change in the contract that will save money and offer better care for your child. Suggest this idea to your health plan. If the first person you talk to says "No," don't stop there. Keep trying by bringing your idea to other people in the company.

Get Help Sorting This All Out

You may still get confused at times as you learn more about health plans. There are a number of people who can help. They include social workers, patient counselors, or people in the clinic business office. And remember your doctor. Doctors who see a lot of children with special health needs may know about paying for their care.

47

Another place to turn is a parents group or support group. People in these groups often know your situation from the inside out: They've been there too. You can get help from their experience and their support.

Plan For The Future

Medical coverage may be fine for your child below the age of 18. But what about coverage beyond that age? Plan ahead now.

With certain health conditions, you may want to establish a guardian for your child. A guardian is someone who has a legal right to make decisions about health care or money matters. The person being cared for is called the ward.

Often a guardianship is set up when a child is disabled and no family member can offer the needed care. The guardianship could start, for example, when the child reaches age 18.

Appointing a guardian is a legal process. Unless you're a lawyer, you'll need some help. You can also talk to a lawyer about setting up a special trust for your child.

CHAPTER 7 / Handling

An Issue

With Your

Health

Plan

When it comes to getting the care your child needs, you may need to be assertive. Stephen Scott and Patricia Siuta, authors of Legal Rights for Developmentally Disabled Persons, *explain why:*

> "Disabled people, as well as their parents or spouses acting on their behalf, often find it difficult to purchase any insurance or adequate insurance at reasonable rates. Some insurance companies consider people with certain disabilities to be too great a risk to insure and have refused to sell them any insurance. Other companies only offer to sell insurance policies at significantly higher rates or sell policies which exclude coverage for the person's disability."

This may be old news to you. What may be real news, however, is that you can get health benefits for your child.

To get the best health care for your child, it helps to:

- *Know how your state regulates health plans*
- *Reach agreements with your health plan or employer up front*
- *Develop a plan for working with your insurer*
- *Support your case when you disagree*
- *Seek out support groups*

Establish An Understanding With Your Health Plan Up Front

Don't wait until things break down and you have to file a complaint. Do something to prevent problems. Following are some of the most important things to do:

◆ Get agreements in writing early on

Before you buy a health plan, get a written statement that it covers the treatments and special equipment your child needs.

We realize this may be hard. You don't always know exactly what your child will need. In fact, those needs can change often in your child's life. Try to forecast your child's needs anyway. Even if your insurer fails to cover all the services you want, you'll know what your benefits are. That way, you can find another source of funds.

Note: The health plan may refuse to give you a written statement pertaining to your particular child *before* he/she is a member. You can request their general list of benefits, however.

◆ Find out what the key words mean

No matter how you receive health insurance—through an HMO, insurance company, self-insured company, or public plan—look for certain terms in your contract. Some of these terms are important to anyone. Others are crucial for parents of a child with special health needs:

- *Who are the **insureds**—that is, the people covered under the policy?*
- *What are the **deductibles**? These are payments you'll have to make out of your own pocket before your insurance will apply.*
- *Are there **copayments**? You may be asked to share in the cost of a covered service or piece of equipment. For*

example, the policy may require you to pay $5.00 for every prescribed medication. Or you might have to pay 35 percent of any mental health services covered under the policy.

- *What are the **exclusions**? These are things the policy does not cover. Read these carefully to see if any service or equipment your child needs is excluded. This section may have another title, such as "Limitations" or "What's Not Covered."*

- *Is there a **pre-existing condition** clause? These deny coverage for an illness or disability that a family member had before the policy began. Or, the policy may cover such a condition, but only after a waiting period. Those waiting periods can vary from one month to several years.*

- *Is there a **cancellation** provision? That is, when can the insurer cancel the policy? Can insurance be cancelled for one or more family members?*

- *What about **renewal**? Can the insurer refuse to renew the policy because of your child's health condition?*

- *Do you find meanings for these terms: **medically necessary services, usual and customary charges, and experimental and investigational treatments**?*

If the plan decides a service is not medically necessary, it may not pay for the service. The same thing can happen if the insurer considers the service too expensive or too risky. Because the contract is a legal document, the plan can refuse to pay for such services. They may never have to pay—even if you take the matter to court. So find out now what these terms mean in your contract. Then decide how they'll affect your family.

◆ Read the actual certificate of coverage

You may have never seen the actual, legally binding contract between you and your health plan. This is often true for members of group plans. Instead, you've probably seen brochures, marketing materials, or other summaries of your policy. However, none of these are legal documents. Only the actual certificate of coverage the insurer gives your company has legal force. Sometimes this is called the "group contract" or the "master policy."

When you research your present plan, or when you want to compare plans, get this certificate. And if you don't understand it, get help from a lawyer or support group.

Let's say that you've researched your health needs, tried to choose the best plan, and stated your needs up front. You and your health plan may still disagree about who should pay for a service your child needs.

This calls for being assertive. Often that means going beyond the first "No" you get from your health plan. To do so, you need to be firm and diplomatic. Most of all, you'll need to be prepared. This section offers ideas on how to do that. For more on assertiveness, see Chapter 2.

Being assertive means developing advocacy skills— not combat skills. Remember that employers may cancel a plan if they feel an employee demands too much. People will respect your knowledge, not your anger. You'll have better chances if you're flexible and willing to listen. After all, you both have the same goal: cost-effective quality care for your child.

Keep in mind that the people at your health plan are not enemies. In many cases, they're also feeling the stress of rising costs.

Above all, be patient. You don't have to be an expert to take the actions we recommend. Instead, you only need to do your homework.

Below are some important points:

◆ Troubleshoot your situation

Watch for signs of trouble. For example, your insurer might take a long time to pay one of your medical bills, or the payment might come late. This could signal a problem.

Find out who to contact from your employer or your insurance company when this happens. Perhaps it is a temporary situation. In any case, it pays to find out soon.

◆ Find out how your request is processed

HMOs and private insurers may process your request differently. This could make a big difference to your family.

With fee-for service insurance, you're probably disputing payment for a service your child has already received. With an HMO, however, your child may still be waiting for the service. Remember that an HMO is often the insurer and the provider of care. This means the service must be approved before the HMO will provide it.

♦ **Find out—in advance and in writing—how your plan handles grievances**

Insurers are required to follow a "fair claims" law. This means they must have a way to process complaints. HMOs have a special system for doing this, and it should be stated in your HMO handbook. In either case, look for the procedure and follow it.

Other plans may not have a clear grievance procedure. You'll have to check your company's policy. Contact your insurance agent or customer service department. If you have a group plan, start with your employer's benefits, personnel, or human resources department.

When it comes to handling consumer complaints, some companies have more red tape than others. Be assertive. But don't proceed before you're sure of the facts. Any person you talk to will have the information on your plan—probably on a computer system. It's also possible your call could go on file. That means it could be used as evidence if you file a complaint.

♦ **When you complain, have all the essential information at hand**

Usually this includes your insurer's name, your policy number, claim number, adjustor or agent's name, and a summary of your complaint. Your insurer will give you more details on what is essential.

♦ **Go directly to the person with responsibility for your case**

The first person who processes your claim may be a customer service representative, a patient counselor, or someone in the member services department. Even though this person takes down the details of your complaint, he or she may not have the final authority to say Yes or No. Ask this person who *does* have authority.

♦ **Do everything you can to move your request through the system**

Handling your request can take a long time. Meanwhile, your child may be waiting for surgery, to see a specialist, or to get a piece of special equipment. Move things along.

There are many ways you can do this. Write "Urgent" on correspondence about your complaint. (This tactic will be less effective if you use it all the time.) Make an appointment to see someone about your request. If nothing happens, follow up every two weeks with another letter or phone call.

Set a reasonable time limit for your insurer to respond, and put it in writing. If the due date passes without a response, get on the phone or write again.

The main point is this: Keep in contact when things don't move forward. When you have to, move "up the ladder." If the person you're talking to is delaying a decision for no reason, talk to that person's supervisor.

It is important to note, if you take legal steps against the plan, this can delay things even more. Exhaust your other options first.

◆ Get all the involved people together

If you and your insurer disagree about coverage, there's probably several parties involved. They could include your child's doctor, your insurance agent, your employer's benefits department, the hospital business office, and more.

Many times, these people never talk directly to each other. Why not change that? Set up a meeting that involves you, your provider, and the insurer's key people. True, this will take energy and time. But these people may agree to meet when they see it's in their best interest to solve a problem. Also, it may be easier for people to agree when they see each other face-to-face.

◆ Choose the right time to file a complaint with a state agency

The procedure for each state varies, but it may be Department of Health or the Department of Commerce. However, it's necessary to pursue all your other options before contacting one of these departments.

◆ Know when to consider a lawsuit

Parents have sued to get health care benefits. This should not be your first strategy, however. Try our other suggestions first. Lawsuits may cost a lot of money—money that comes from the same pool as your health care benefits. Lawsuits can also lead to long delays with no positive results. Besides, there's no guarantee you will win.

Sometimes parents feel they have to sue—especially when their child's life is threatened by lack of funds to pay for care. Before you sue, get good legal advice. Your source could be a private lawyer or a legal advocacy group

Document By Maintaining A "Paper Trail"

As you work to get the care your child needs, create a "paper trail." Get all agreements and decisions that affect your child in writing. Also, keep careful notes on key conversations and meetings.

This is what's meant by "documenting" your case. To have any case at all, you've got to document. When you're without documentation, you're without a case.

The following are suggestions for getting the documentation you need:

◆ **Keep a pen and notebook handy**

Be prepared to take notes when you have to. That means keeping pen and paper in key places: by the phone, in your car, at your job, and in your purse or briefcase.

Be ready to write down ideas at odd times. You may get ideas when getting dressed in the morning, between appointments, in waiting rooms, riding to work, or going on a trip. Collect all your notes in a one place and organize them into file folders. If you have access to a personal computer, you may want to use it to keep your records.

◆ **Keep notes on phone conversations**

Who did you talk to? When? What did you say, and what did the other person say? Did you decide anything or agree on anything? Take careful notes that answer all these questions.

◆ **Send a follow-up letter**

After your phone conversation, send a letter to the person you talked with. Sum up your conversation, and list each agreement or decision reached. Be sure to sign your letter.

At the end of your letter, include a statement such as this:

This is my understanding of our phone conversation. If you do not agree, or if you want to add any points, please contact me in five working days. If I haven't heard from you by then, I will assume you agree with this letter.

Why go to all this trouble? Because you have more interest in your child's case than people who are involved with many other children. Also, verbal agreements don't count.

Unless it's in writing, your case won't hold up at a hearing or in court.

One final note: Always keep extra copies of your letters in your personal files.

◆ Take careful notes at all meetings

Here you can follow many of the same ideas for phone conversations. Write up minutes of the meeting. Sign and date them.

Again, list all the agreements reached and the decisions made. Note any follow up actions people said they'd take. Then, at the top or bottom of your minutes, include a sentence like this:

This is my understanding of our discussion. If you do not agree, or if you want to add any points, please contact me in five working days. If I haven't heard from you by then, I will assume you agree with this document.

See that every person present at the meeting gets a copy. Again, keep extra copies of meeting minutes in your files.

◆ Send copies of your letters or minutes to your contact's supervisors

In making your case, you may be in constant contact with one person at the insurance company or HMO. Is this person acting on your complaint? Or is the process taking too long? Are you being blocked or intimidated? In this situation, you can take action.

One thing to do is send a letter to your contact's supervisor. Then the next time you call or write your contact, mention that you've sent this letter.

◆ Keep copies of all letters, minutes, and documents relating to your case

It's too easy to lose track of these important papers. Keep them handy, and file them in a way that helps you to find things quickly. File letters, for example, in order by date; or alphabetically by subject. On each letter, note how you responded or what action your insurer took. Also, keep these papers in one central place. Set aside space on your desk, in a file cabinet, or other storage area.

◆ **Keep a log of what insurance claims are pending and which are paid**

This is important if you have fee-for-service insurance, and when your child uses many medical services. If your insurer delays paying a claim, you don't want to be responsible for it. Keep the company on its toes.

◆ **Ask your doctor to use the language of the plan contract**

The health plan may ask your doctor or hospital to confirm that your child needs a certain treatment. Explain this to your doctor, and give him or her a copy of your policy or contract. When writing the letter, ask your doctor to use the same language used in the policy. For example, your policy may say that speech therapy is covered only when "medically necessary." It can help if your doctor uses this term and explains why the treatment is medically necessary.

◆ **Add more details to build your case**

When writing to your insurer, explain in detail why this treatment is needed or why your child needs that piece of equipment. Also explain what will happen if your claim is denied.

It is helpful to include other details too. Attach articles from medical literature showing that the treatment is "usual and customary." This may take real effort, but it will pay off if the insurer agrees to your claim. Ask your doctor or hospital for help.

PART 3 / Where
To Find
More
Help

For
Further
Reading

In addition to checking the materials listed here, write the Association for the Care of Children's Health. This group offers books, pamphlets, and videotapes about children with special needs. It also has a list of parents you can contact. The address:

Association for the Care of Children's Health (ACCH)
7910 Woodmont Avenue
Suite 300
Bethesda, MD 20014

A good source of information, materials, and parent training is:

Federation For Children With Special Needs
312 Stuart Street
Boston, MA 02116
(617) 482-2915
(National Network of Parents Coalition)

◆ Recommended Publications

A Guide to Health Care Coverage for the Child with a Chronic Illness or Disability: A Funding Source Catalog for Wisconsin, 1988. Gaylord, Catherine L. and Leonard, Alice M.

Available from the Center for Public Representation, 520 University Avenue South, Madison, WI 53703.

A Parent Guide For Doctors Visits, 1987. Connecticut Developmental Disabilities Council. Available from Connecticut Developmental Disabilities Council, 90 Pitkin Street, East Hartford, CT 06108.

Alternatives: A Family Guide to Legal and Financial Planning for the Disabled. Russell, L. Mark. Evanston, IL: First Publications, 1983, P.O. Box 1832, Evanston, IL 60204.

Consumer's Guide to Health Care Plans, Twin Cities Metropolitan Area, January 1985. Metropolitan Council and Metropolitan Health Planning Board. Available from the Metropolitan Council, 300 Metro Square Building, 7th and Robert Streets, St. Paul, MN 55101.

Directory of Early Childhood/Early Intervention Services for the State of Minnesota, 1989. Available from PACER Center, Inc., 4826 Chicago Avenue South, Minneapolis, MN 55417-1055, (612) 827-2966, voice and TDD, 1-800-53PACER, toll-free for long distance calls.

Early Intervention: Building Blocks For The Future, 1989; revised 1990. Trimbach, Kathy, Abderholden, Sue and Karen Grykiewicz. Available from Association for Retarded Citizens of Minnesota, 3225 Lyndale Avenue South, Minneapolis, MN 55404, (612) 827-5641 or 1-800-582-5256.

Health Care Coverage and Your Disabled Child: A Guide for Parents, 1983. United Cerebral Palsy of Minnesota. Available from United Cerebral Palsy of Minnesota, 1821 University Avenue, St. Paul, MN 55014.

How To Develop a Community Network, 1987. Pathfinder. Available from Pathfinder, 2324 University Avenue W., St. Paul, MN 55114.

How To Get Services By Being Assertive, 1985. Des Jardins, Charlotte. Available from the Coordinating Council for Handicapped Children, 220 South State, Chicago, IL 60604.

Legal Rights of Developmentally Disabled Persons: An Advocacy Manual for Minnesota, 1979. Scott, Stephen and Siuta, Patricia. Available from Legal Advocacy for Developmentally Disabled Persons In Minnesota, 222 Grain Exchange Building, 323 Fourth Avenue So., Minneapolis, MN 55415.

Making Your Medical Decisions. Hosford, Bowen. New York: Ungar, 1987. Available from Harper and Row, Keystone Industrial Park, Scranton, PA 18512.

Managing the School Age Child with a Chronic Health Condition. Larson, Georgianna, ed. Minneapolis, MN: DCI Publishing, 1988. Available from Pathfinder Resources, 2324 University Avenue W., Minneapolis, MN 55114.

Meeting the Medical Bills (videotape). National Center for Clinical Infant Programs. Available from the National Center for Clinical Infant Programs, 2000 14th Street N., Suite 380, Arlington, VA 22201-2500, (703) 528-4300.

Quality Health Care for People with Developmental Disabilities: A Guide for Parents and Other Caregivers, 1988. Pfaffinger, Kathleen M. and Nelson, Richard P. Available from Minnesota University Affiliated Program on Developmental Disabilities, University of Minnesota, 6 Pattee Hall, 150 Pillsbury Drive S.E., Minneapolis, MN 55455.

The Exceptional Parent Magazine. For subscriptions, write to Exceptional Parent, 605 Commonwealth Avenue, Boston, MA 02215.

Thoughts About My Child, 1988, revised 1989. Also available in Spanish and Hmong. Cost: $.85, includes postage. Available from PACER Center, Inc., 4826 Chicago Avenue South, Minneapolis, MN 55417-1055, (612) 827-2966, voice and TDD, 1-800-53PACER, toll-free for long distance calls.

Understanding Your Health Insurance Options: A Guide for Families Who Have Children With Special Health Care Needs. McManus, Margaret A. Washington, D.C.: 1988, Association for the Care of Children's Health, 3615 Wisconsin Avenue N.W. Washington, DC 20016.

National
Organizations
And
Agencies

Alexander Graham Bell Association For The Deaf
3416 Volta Place N.W.
Washington, DC 20007
(202) 337-5220

American Association On Mental Retardation
1719 Kalorama Rd. N.W.
Washington, DC 20009-2684
(202) 387-1968
Toll-free: 1-800-424-3688

American Association Of University Affiliated Programs For Persons With Developmental Disabilities
Suite 406
605 Cameron St.
Silver Springs, MD 20910
(301) 588-8252

American Council Of The Blind
1010 Vermont Avenue N.W., Suite 1100
Washington, DC 20005
(202) 393-3666

American Federation For The Blind
15 W. 16th Street
New York, NY 10011
(212) 620-2000

American Speech-Language-Hearing Association
10801 Rockville Pike
Rockville, MD 20852
(301) 897-5700

Association For Children And Adults With Learning Disabilities
4156 Library Road
Pittsburgh, PA 15234
(412) 341-1515

Association For The Care Of Children's Health
7910 Woodmont Avenue
Suite 300
Bethesda, MD 20014

Better Hearing Institute Hearing Helpline
P.O. Box 1840
Washington, DC 20013
Toll-free: 1-800-424-8576

Cancer Information Service
(800)-4-CANCER (National Line)

Center For Law And Education
Larsen Hall, 6th Floor
14 Appian Way
Cambridge, MA 02138
(617) 495-4666

Child And Adolescent Family Support Branch
National Institute Of Mental Health (NIMH)
Room 7C-14
5600 Fishers Lane
Rockville, MD 20851
(301) 443-1333

Children's Defense Fund
122 C Street N.W.
Washington, DC 20001
(202) 628-8787

Council For Exceptional Children (CEC)
1920 Association Drive
Reston, VA 22091
(703) 620-3660

Disability Rights Education And Defense Fund (DREDF)
2212 6th Street
Berkeley, CA 94710
(415) 644-2555

Epilepsy Foundation Of America
4351 Garden City Drive
Suite 406
Landover, MD 20785
(301) 459-3700

ERIC Clearinghouse On Adult Career & Vocational Education
1960 Kenny Road
Columbus, OH 43210
(800) 848-4815

ERIC Clearinghouse On Handicapped And Gifted Children
1920 Association Dr.
Reston, VA 22091
(703) 620-3660
Fax: (703) 264-9494

Federation For Children With Special Needs
312 Stuart Street
Boston, MA 02116
(617) 482-2915
(National Network Of Parents Coalition)

Health Insurance Association Of America
1850 K St. N.W.
Washington, DC 20006
(202) 862-4063

Human Growth Foundation
4720 Montgomery Lane
Bethesda, MD 20814
(301) 656-7540.
Toll-free: 1-800-451-6434

Leukemia Society Of America
733 Third Ave., New York, NY 10017
(212) 573-8484

LINC Resources, Inc.
3857 N. High St.
Columbus, OH 43214
(614) 263-5462
(Information Center For Special Education Media
And Materials)

Lowe's Syndrome Association
222 Lincoln St.
West Lafayette, IN 47906
(317) 743-3634

Lupus Foundation Of America, Inc.
1717 Massachusetts Avenue N.W., Suite 203
Washington, DC 20036
1-800-558-0121

March Of Dimes Birth Defects Foundation
1275 Mamaroneck Avenue
White Plains, NY 10605

Mental Health Law Project
2021 L Street N.W., 8th Floor
Washington, DC 20036
(202) 467-5730

Mexican-American Legal Defense Fund
604 Mission St., 10th Floor
San Francisco, CA 94105
(415) 543-5598

National Alliance For The Mentally Ill
2101 Wilson Blvd., Suite 302
Arlington, VA 22201
(703) 524-7600

National Association Of The Deaf
814 Thayer Avenue
Silver Springs, MD 20910
(301) 587-1788

National Association For Retarded Citizens
2501 Avenue J
Arlington, TX 76006
(817) 640-0204

National Association Of State Directors Of Special Education
2021 K. St. N.W., Suite 315
Washington, DC 20006
(202) 296-1800

National Center For Clinical Infant Programs
2000 14th Street N., Suite 380
Arlington, VA 22201-2500
(703) 528-4300

National Center For Education In Maternal And Child Health (NCEMCH)
38th & R Streets N.W.
Washington, DC 20057
(202) 625-8400

National Center For Law And The Deaf
800 Florida Avenue N.E.
Washington, DC 20002
(202) 651-5454

National Center For Stuttering
200 E. 33rd Street
New York City, NY 10016
(800) 221-2483

National Council On The Handicapped
800 Independence Ave. S.W., Suite 814
Washington, DC 20591
(202) 267-3846

National Down Syndrome Congress
1800 Dempster Street
Parkridge, IL 60068-1146
1-800-232-NDSC

National Down Syndrome Society
141 5th Avenue
New York City, NY 10010
Toll-free: 1-800-221-4602

National Easter Seal Society
70 E. Lake St.
Chicago, IL 60601
(312) 726-6200

National Federation Of The Blind
655 15th Street N.W., Suite 300
Washington, DC 20005
(202) 639-4028

National Head Injury Foundation
333 Turnpike Rd.
Southboro, MA 01772
Toll-free: 1-800-444-6443

National Health Information Center
P.O. Box 1133
Washington, DC 20013-1133
Toll-free: 1-800-336-4797

National Hearing Aid Society
20361 Middle Belt Road
Livonia, MI 48152
Toll-free: 1-800-521-5247

**National Information Center For Handicapped
Children And Youth (NICHNY)**
Mail Address: P. O. Box 1492
Washington, DC 20013
Business Address: Suite 1100
7926 Jones Branch Dr.
McClean, VA 22102
(703) 893-6061

**National Library Service For The Blind And
Physically Handicapped**
The Library Of Congress
Washington, DC 20542
(202) 707-5100

National Mental Health Association
1021 Prince Street
Alexandria, VA 22314
(703) 684-7722

National Network Of Parent Centers
Suite 1112
1522 K St. N.W.
Washington, DC 20005
(603) 224-7005, Voice and TDD

**National Organization For Albinism And
Hypopigmentation (NOAH)**
Suite 1816
1500 Locust St.
Philadelphia, PA 19102
(215) 545-2322

National Organization For Rare Diseases
P. O. Box 8923
New Fairfield, CT 06812
(203) 746-6518

National Resource Institute On Children With Handicaps (NRICH)
University Of Washington
Mail Stop WJ-10
Seattle, WA 98195
(206) 543-2254

National Spinal Cord Injury Association
369 Elliot Street
Newton Upper Falls, MA 02164

Office Of Civil Rights
National Office
Department Of Education
400 Maryland Avenue S.W.
Room 5000
Switzer Building
Washington, DC 20202

Office Of Civil Rights
Region 5 Office
Department Of Education
Room 700C
401 S. State St.
Chicago, IL 60605
(312) 886-3456

Office Of Special Education
And Rehabilitative Services (OSERS)
Room 3018 Switzer Building
330 C St. S.W.
Washington, DC 20202
(202) 732-1723

Resource Access Project (RAP)
240 Col. Wolfe School
403 E. Healey
Champaign, IL 61820
(217) 333-3876
(Network For Head Start)

SKIP (Sick Kids Need Involved People, Inc.)
National Headquarters
216 Newport Drive
Severna Park, MD 21146
(301) 647-0164

Spina Bifida Association Of America
1700 Rockville Pike
Suite 540
Rockville, MD 20852
(301) 770-7222
Hotline: 1-800-621-3141

Task Force On The Rights And Empowerment Of Americans With Disabilities
Suite 516C
907 6th St. S.W.
Washington, DC 20024
(202) 488-7684
(202) 484-1370 TDD

The Association For Persons With Severe Handicaps (TASH)
7010 Roosevelt Way N.E.
Seattle, WA 98115
(206) 523-8446

United Cerebral Palsy Association
66 E. 34th Street
New York, NY 10016
(212) 481-6300

World Institute On Disability
Suite 4
1720 Oregon St.
Berkeley, CA 94703
(415) 486-8314

Glossary

Acute care. Medical care provided in direct response to an illness, injury, or other condition. Acute care contrasts with preventive care, which tries to reduce the chances of acquiring a condition.

Adoption subsidies. Programs that pay some medical costs for some adopted children with special health needs. To qualify, these children must be from the United States. Even with this subsidy, the family may still qualify for Medical Assistance.

Advocacy group. An organization that serves parents and children with a specific health care need. The group might provide training for parents, funding for health care, counseling, or support groups. Some advocacy groups lobby for legislation to benefit the people they serve.

Cancellation. The clause in an insurance policy that explains how you, or the insurer, can end coverage under the policy.

Certificate of coverage. In a group health insurance policy, this is the legally binding contract between the employer and the insurer. Employees enrolled in the plan may receive individual certificates or summary descriptions of this contract. These documents for individuals may not be legally binding.

Combination plans. Some policies include features from fee-for-service insurance and prepaid (HMO) plans. For example, the combination plan may offer HMO-type benefits if you see one of its doctors. If you see a doctor who's not part of the plan, you may have copayments and deductibles to pay.

Coordination of benefits. A clause found in most insurance policies that states what will happen when two or more insurers cover the same service—what happens when coverage "overlaps." In these cases, one type of insurance may be primary, which means that it is first to pay for the covered service. Or, each insurer may pay part of the covered cost.

Continuation. The clause in a group insurance policy that states how you can extend your coverage on a temporary basis. This allows you to keep getting insurance at group rates—for a certain number of months—if the group policy is cancelled. The employer usually will not pay part of the premium for you, which means you will have to pay the full premium to continue the policy.

Conversion. The clause in a group insurance policy that states how you can change your group coverage to individual coverage. You might decide to convert your policy if you leave your present job, for example. Usually you will have to pay the full premium for the individual policy. The employer will not pay part of the premium for you.

Copayments. Some insurance policies will "split" the cost of a covered service with you. For example, the insurer may pay up to 80 percent of the cost of seeing a psychiatrist; you must pay the remaining 20 percent. The amount you're responsible for is called the copayment.

Deductibles. The amount you must pay before your insurance starts paying benefits. For example, each year you may have to pay the first $250 of covered medical costs for each member of your family; your insurance benefits apply for amounts above $250.

Documenting. Keeping written records relating to your family's medical care and insurance. You may need detailed records to support your case if you disagree with your insurer.

Due process. One of the rights granted to you by federal law (PL 94-142). You have a right to challenge any decision that affects your child's education. You can make your case by getting an independent evaluation, a hearing from a neutral authority (the due process hearing), an appeal of the hearing results, other formal complaints, or a lawsuit.

Endorsement. An attachment to an insurance policy. The endorsement extends or limits the coverage provided by the policy. Endorsements are also called riders.

Exclusions. The part of the insurance contract that states what is not covered under the policy.

Experimental and investigational treatments. Insurers consider some treatments too unusual or too rare and often will not pay for them. Your policy will define these procedures in general terms. It's important that you find out exactly what these treatments are.

Fee-for-service insurance. A type of health insurance that pays health care providers on the basis of each service they give. With this insurance, you often have a wider choice of providers than with HMOs. However, some services are not covered, and there are usually deductibles and copayments.

Grace period. Premiums for an insurance policy are due on a certain date. Often you can pay the premium up to a certain number of days after the due date. That number of days is the grace period.

Group policy. An insurance plan that provides benefits to more than one person or family. Group plans are offered as benefits from employers, labor unions, and credit unions. Usually your costs for a group plan are lower than costs for a similar individual plan.

Guardianship. A person who has legal duty to make decisions that affect another person. Those decisions can relate to health care, finances, housing, and other areas of life. The person responsible for care is called the guardian, and the person cared for is called the ward.

Health Maintenance Organization. A health insurance plan that offers many inpatient and outpatient services for a fixed premium. To receive full benefits, you must see providers who are part of the HMO.

Health plan. As used in this book, any program that helps pay for health care. One example is a traditional insurance plan. Others are HMOs, PPOs, and public program such as Medicaid.

Hill-Burton Program. The Hill-Burton Act provides federal funds to modernize hospitals and other medical facilities. To get these funds, the facility must provide some free or low-cost care to people who cannot afford to pay. Funds under this program are limited.

HMO. See Health Maintenance Organization

Individual policy. An insurance plan that offers benefits to one person or family. This contrasts with group coverage.

Inpatient care. Medical services that are provided along with lodging and meals. Often this word refers to hospital care.

Insured. Any person who receives benefits under an insurance policy.

Limitations. The clause in an insurance policy that states what services are not covered—or services that are covered only in part.

Mandated benefits. Federal or state law requires health insurers to provide certain kinds of coverage in the policies they sell. These are mandated benefits. Mandated benefits are different for HMOs than for other private insurers.

Medicaid. A health insurance plan funded by the federal, state, and county governments. It serves people who receive AFDC and others who are blind, disabled, under 21, or over age 65. Also called MA or Medical Assistance.

Medicaid waivers. Programs that relax some of the require-ments for who can receive Medical Assistance, and for what services can be covered. These programs provide services in the home and community for people who would otherwise be in institutions.

Medically necessary services. A clause in a health insurance policy that states that the policy only covers services needed to maintain a certain level of health. The clause also defines—often in general terms—what those services are. Be sure to find out exactly what your insurer means by this term.

MR/RC Waiver. A special program under Medicaid. It allows certain children to be eligible for Medicaid, based on the child's income and assets. The child can get all services covered under Medicaid and other services that prevent stays in an institution.

Open enrollment. An option that allows you to sign up for an insurance plan without having to fill out an application. Often this means you do not have to provide any details about your health or the health of your family members.

Outpatient care. Medical care that's provided outside a hospital or other residential program. Examples of outpatient care are visits to a doctor's office or a dentist.

PPO. See Preferred Provider Organization

Pre-existing condition. A health condition that's present before health insurance takes effect. These conditions are listed in the policy. There may be no coverage for the condi-tion; or, you may have to wait a certain period before coverage applies to the condition.

Preferred Provider Organizations (PPOs). A prepaid plan that gives you a financial incentive to see certain providers. If you see a provider who's not on this list, you may have extra costs to pay.

Prepaid plans. A health insurance plan where you pay a fixed premium to cover much of the care you receive. Prepaid plans include Health Maintenance Organizations (HMOs) and Preferred Provider Organizations (PPOs).

Premium. The amount that must be paid to keep an insurance policy in force. There may be other costs with the policy, such as deductibles and copayments.

Preventive care. Medical services that try to reduce the chances of an illness, injury, or other condition. This contrasts with acute care, which is given after the condition has occurred.

Private insurance. Plans offered by health maintenance organizations, preferred provider organizations, other insurance companies, and self-insured companies. In contrast, public plans are funded by federal, state, or local governments.

Provider. Any person who provides medical care or medical equipment. Providers include doctors, hospitals, nurses, therapists, and dentists. The provider who has the main responsibility for your family's care is called your primary provider. Providers are also called health care providers.

Public plans. Insurance plans that are funded—at least in part—by federal, state, or local governments. Examples of public plans are Medical Assistance and Medicare.

Referral. Seeing a doctor, nurse, or therapist for a special reason. Referrals are set up and approved by your regular doctor.

Renewal. A clause in an insurance policy that states how you or the insurer can keep the policy in force after initial coverage expires.

Rider. An attachment to an insurance policy. The rider extends or limits the coverage provided by the policy. Riders are also called endorsements.

Self-insured plan. Medical benefits that are paid for out of a company's own funds. This contrasts with paying premiums to an outside insurer for those benefits. However, self-insured plans may be administered by an outside company.

Traditional insurance. A type of health insurance that pays health care providers on the basis of each service they give. With this insurance, you often have a wider choice of providers than with HMOs. However, some services are not covered, and there are usually deductibles and copayments.

Usual and customary charges. Fees for medical services that the insurer considers reasonable. If a fee goes above that amount, the insurer may not pay for it. Each insurer determines what usual and customary charges are. Be sure to find out how your insurer does this.

Waiting period. Health plans may provide coverage for an illness or chronic condition only after a certain amount of time has passed. That time is called the waiting period. Waiting periods vary from six months to several years.

Waiver. A special state Medicaid program that provides home and community-based services to people with chronic health conditions or disabilities who would otherwise need to live in an institution. Examples of such institutions are intermediate care facilities (ICFs), nursing homes or hospitals. Waiver programs provide basic Medicaid services plus special program services such as case management.

Part 4 / Special
Resources
For Your Child

Finding Help In Your State

The health plans discussed in this book are available in many states. In addition, your state may offer special programs, both public and private. To learn about resources available in your state, one of your first calls should be to your state program for Children with Special Health Care Needs (CSHCN). There is a list of these state CSHCN programs on pages 86-88.

As you get information about programs available in your state, be sure to ask the following questions as a first step:

- *Who is eligible*
- *Limitations (who is not eligible for the program, or what it will not cover)*
- *Types of services covered*
- *Who to contact*

Another important contact will be your state's Medicaid agency. Many states have Medicaid waivers that "relax" some of the eligibility requirements of Medicaid. There may be a number of waivers available in your state, so be sure to ask questions about who is eligible, types of services covered and who to contact regarding each waiver.

After making these initial contacts, you will probably have a list of agencies and organizations to contact regarding progress. Your main purpose in making these calls will be to find out whether your child is eligible for any of the programs. This may seem a daunting task, but planning ahead and sitting down with a pad of paper, a pencil, and a list of questions will make the task easier. It is helpful to jot down notes during your phone contact, particularly noting the name of the individual you spoke with so you will know who to contact if you have additional questions.

Questions To Ask About Any Program

When you contact a program, ask questions to get the information you need. Here's a list of questions to start with. You might want to copy it and post it near your phone.

- *How do I apply?*
- *Do I need to have my application in by a certain date?*
- *Who will review my application?*
- *How long does it take to process my application?*
- *Is there a copay?*
- *Can I get a complete list of covered services?*
- *What services are not covered under this program?*
- *How long would my child be covered under this program?*
- *Who will screen my child for services?*
- *Will someone write out a plan for my child's care? This plan might be called an Individual Service Plan (ISP) or something similar.*
- *Will someone coordinate my child's care?*
- *Do I need a case manager to take part in this program?*
- *How will this program affect our current health insurance?*
- *If I disagree with a decision about my child's care, what can I do? Ask about the appeal process.*
- *What information can you send me about this program?*

As you start contacting programs, you'll think of more things to ask.

You may feel overwhelmed by all the information you get. Don't be discouraged. Just remember to ask questions, and keep asking until you understand the answers.

Additional Sources Of Information

Each state will have many good sources of information on services for children with special needs. Your county social service agency should be able to assist you in finding options available in your area. You can also check with the social services department of your local children's hospital. Your state Department of Health, Department of Human Services (Welfare) and Department of Education may be able to answer questions or direct you to someone who can.

In addition, most states have advocacy groups or organizations directed toward specific disabilities, e.g., diabetes, spina bifida, epilepsy associations. These organizations can frequently put you in touch with support groups or answer questions about services available for a child with a specific health condition. You may find these organizations in the yellow pages of your phone book by looking up the specific health condition. Your physician or case manager may also have a list of groups that serve children with special health care needs.

Understanding How Health Plans Are Regulated In Your State

Health plans must follow laws and regulations when they do business. This gives you some options to lobby for the health care your child needs.

If you have a complaint about your health insurance, you should contact the insurance commissioner in the Department of Commerce in your state. This department looks at complaints from consumers about their insurance and can take action against a company suspected of fraud. The Department of Commerce cannot, however, order a health plan to pay; only the courts can do that. The Department of Commerce should also have records that track insurance companies to see that they're solvent and have enough money to pay claims.

Health maintenance organizations (HMO) may be regulated by another agency in your state, e.g., the Department of Health. Your state insurance commissioner will be able to direct you to the correct agency.

Note: Self-insured companies are not regulated by the state. That's because of a federal law—the Employee Retirement Income Security Act (ERISA). According to ERISA, the federal government regulates employee benefit plans. This includes plans offered by self-insured companies. Even though they fall outside state law, most large self-insured plans offer benefits that compare well with other plans.

Resources For Families Without Health Insurance

This book has described many public and private health plan options for children with special health needs and their families. But some children have no insurance. There are a variety of reasons why this situation occurs. Children with special needs may be excluded from obtaining insurance due to pre-existing conditions or insurance-plan riders. Some states have special high risk pools (see page 85) for people who cannot otherwise obtain private insurance. But these risk share programs may have high premiums, deductibles and copays, which can make this option too expensive for some families. Medicaid is a public sector option for children with special needs, but parental income and assets can make this option impossible due to income spend-downs needed to qualify for a Medicaid "medically-needy" option (see pages 34-36).

What can a family do if they and/or their child has no insurance? The situation is certainly discouraging, but careful research may uncover hidden options. Here are some suggested programs/options to explore:

◆ **State Title V Programs**

These programs, also known as Children with Special Health Care Needs (CSHCN) programs, vary from state to state. They often provide diagnostic services and reimbursement for inpatient and outpatient treatment (prior approval and program eligibility necessary). Some programs will pay insurance premiums, deductibles and co-pays for eligible families.

◆ **Special Medicaid Waivers**

To address the needs of children and adults with special health needs, many states have developed special

Medicaid programs called Medicaid waivers. These programs are useful to families who find that their income and assets keep them from qualifying for regular Medicaid programs. Check with your state Medicaid agency for more information on your state's programs.

◆ **State High Risk Pools**

Some states provide a special high risk insurance program for children and adults who cannot qualify for regular insurance due to their special health needs. Contact your insurance commissioner's office to see if your state has a high risk insurance program.

◆ **Hospital Hill-Burton Fund Programs**

The Hill-Burton Act is a law that provides federal funds to build and modernize health facilities, such as hospitals. In order to receive these funds, the facility must agree to provide a certain amount of free care to people who cannot afford to pay, or it must provide that care at a reduced cost. Funds under this program are limited. To find out if your hospital or clinic offers this program, call 1-800-638-0742.

◆ **Sliding-fee Scale Payments**

Some hospitals, clinics and physician's offices will make special payment allowances for families who do not have insurance. It is best to check **before** your child uses the service. Ask about sliding-fee scale (payment based on income level) or special monthly payment programs.

◆ **Disability Organizations (see pages 64-71)**

Some disability organizations can provide financial support for families. They may be able to assist in purchasing certain items, such as wheelchairs or computers.

Where To Find These Public And Private Programs

If your child with special needs does not have health insurance coverage, the following people and agencies may have information on private and public programs in your state that can help you:

- *your child's physician or nurse practitioner*
- *your child's school nurse or special education teacher*
- *the Children with Special Health Care Needs (CSHCN) program in your state, also know as the State Title V Program (see pages 86-88)*

The federal government requires each state to have a program for Children with Special Health Care Needs (CSHCN). This agency is often referred to as the Title V Program. Your CSHCN office will be an excellent source of information on resources and financing of clinical and rehabilitative services. In addition, CSHCN offices often provide services for eligible families.

Alabama CSHCN Program
Division of Rehabilitative &
Crippled Children's Services
2129 East South Building
Montgomery, AL 36111

Alaska CSHCN Program
Handicapped Children's Program
Section of Family Health
Department of Health & Social
Services
1231 Gambell Street
Anchorage, AK 99501

Arizona CSHCN Program
Office of Children's Rehabilitative
Services
Arizona Department of Health
1740 W. Adam, Room 205
Phoenix, AZ 85007

Arkansas CSHCN Program
Arkansas Children's Medical
Services
Division of Economic & Medical
Services
P.O. Box 1437
Little Rock, AR 72203

California CSHCN Program
California Children Services
Branch
State Department of Health
714 "P" Street, Room 323
Sacramento, CA 95814

Colorado CSHCN Program
Handicapped Children's Program
Colorado Department of Health
4210 East 11th Avenue
Denver, CO 80220

Connecticut CSHCN Program
Health Services for Handicapped
Children Section
Department of Health Services
150 Washington Street
Hartford, CT 06106

Delaware CSHCN Program
Handicapped Children's Services
Bureau of Personal Health Services
Division of Public Health
P.O. Box 637
Dover, DE 19903

District of Columbia CSHCN Program
Bureau of Maternal and Child
Health
D.C. Department of Human
Services
1660 L. Street, N.W.
Washington, DC 20036

Florida CSHCN Program
Children's Medical Services
Program Office
Department of Health & Rehabilitative Services
1317 Winewood Blvd.
Tallahassee, FL 32301

Georgia CSHCN Program
Children's Medical Services
Georgia Department of Human
Resources
878 Peachtree St., N.E., Suite 214
Atlanta, GA 30309

Hawaii CSHCN Program
Children with Special Health Needs
Branch
741 Sunset Avenue
Honolulu, HI 96816

Idaho CSHCN Program
Children's Special Health Program
Department of Health and Welfare
Statehouse
Boise, ID 83720

Illinois CSHCN Program
The University of Illinois at
Chicago
Division of Services for Crippled
Children
2040 Hill Meadows Drive, Suite A
Springfield, IL 62702-4698

Indiana CSHCN Program
Division of Services for Crippled
Children
Department of Public Welfare
238 South Meridian Street
Indianapolis, IN 46225

Iowa CSHCN Program
Child Health Specialty Clinics
250 Hospital School Building
University of Iowa
Iowa City, IA 52242

Kansas CSHCN Program
Crippled Children's Program
Kansas Department of Health &
Environment
Forbes Field #740
Topeka, KS 66612

Kentucky CSHCN Program
Commission for Handicapped
Children
982 Eastern Parkway
Louisville, KY 40217

Louisiana CSHCN Program
Handicapped Children's Services
Office of Health Services &
Environmental Quality
Department of Health & Human
Resources
P.O. Box 60630
New Orleans, LA 70160

Maine CSHCN Program
Department of Human Services
Augusta, ME 04333

Maryland CSHCN Program
Children's Medical Services
201 West Preston Street
Room 421
Baltimore, MD 21201

Massachusetts CSHCN Program
Division of Programs for Children
with Special Health Care Needs
Bureau of Parent, Child &
Adolescent Health Programs
Massachusetts Department of
Public Health
150 Tremont Street, 4th Floor
Boston, MA 02111

Michigan CSHCN Program
Division of Services to Crippled
Children
Bureau of Community Services
Michigan Department of Public
Health
3023 North Logan
P.O. Box 30035
Lansing, MI 48909

Minnesota CSHCN Program
Services for Children w/Handicaps
Department of Health
717 S.E. Delaware St.
P.O. Box 9441
Minneapolis, MN 55440

Mississippi CSHCN Program
Children's Medical Program
Mississippi State Department of
Health
P.O. Box 1700
Jackson, MS 39215-1700

Missouri CSHCN Program
Bureau of Special Health Care
Needs
P.O. Box 570
Jefferson City, MO 65102

Montana CSHCN Program
Bureau of Maternal & Child Health
Cogswell Building
Helena, MT 59620

Nebraska CSHCN Program
Department of Social Services
P.O. Box 95026
Lincoln, NE 68509-5026

Nevada CSHCN Program
Family Health Services
Nevada Health Division
Department of Human Resources
Room 200, Kinkead Building
505 E. King Street
Carson City, NV 89710

New Hampshire CSHCN Program
Bureau for Handicapped Children
Division of Public Health Services
Health & Welfare Building
6 Hazen Drive
Concord, NH 03301

New Jersey CSHCN Program
Special Child Health Services
New Jersey State Department of
Health/CN 364
Trenton NJ 08625

New Mexico CSHCN Program
Children's Medical Service
P.O. Box 968
Santa Fe, NM 87504-0968

New York CSHCN Program
Special Children Services
Bureau of Maternal, Child &
Adolescent Health
New York State Dept. of Health
Empire State Plaza
Corning Tower Building, Room 821
Albany, NY 12237

North Carolina CSHCN Program
Crippled Children's Program
Department of Human Resources
P.O. Box 2091
Raleigh, NC 27602

North Dakota CSHCN Program
Crippled Children's Services
Department of Human Services
State Capitol
Bismarck, ND 58505

Ohio CSHCN Program
Bureau of Crippled Children's
Services
Ohio Department of Public Health
P.O. Box 118 / 7th Floor
246 North High Street
Columbus, OH 43266-0118

Oklahoma CSHCN Program
Department of Human Services
P.O. Box 25352
Oklahoma City, OK 73125

Oregon CSHCN Program
Crippled Children's Division
Oregon Health Sciences University
3181 S.W. Sam Jackson Road
Portland, OR 97201

Pennsylvania CSHCN Program
Division of Rehabilitation
Department of Health
714 Health & Welfare Building
Harrisburg, PA 17108

Rhode Island CSHCN Program
Division of Family Health
Rhode Island Department of Health
Room 302, 75 Davis Street
Providence, RI 02908

South Carolina CSHCN Program
Division of Children's Health (Inc.
CC)
Department of Health & Environ-
mental Control
2600 Bull Street
Columbia, SC 29201

South Dakota CSHCN Program
Children's Comprehensive Health
South Dakota State Department of
Health
Joe Foss Building, Room 313
523 East Capitol Street
Pierre, SD 57501

Tennessee CSHCN Program
Crippled Children's Services
Tennessee Department of Health &
Environment
100 Ninth Avenue, North
Nashville, TN 37219-5405

Texas CSHCN Program
Chronically Ill & Disabled
Children's Services
Texas Department of Health
1100 West 49th Street
Austin, TX 78756

Utah CSHCN Program
Handicapped Children's Services
Bureau
Division of Health
P.O. Box 16650
288 N. 1460 West
Salt Lake City, UT 84116-0650

Vermont CSHCN Program
Handicapped Children's Services
Vermont Department of Health
P.O. Box 70
1193 North Avenue
Burlington, VT 05402

Virginia CSHCN Program
Division of Children's Specialty
Services
State Department of Health
109 Governor Street
Richmond, VA 23219

Washington CSHCN Program
Bureau for Parent and Child Health
Services
Department of Social and Health
Services
Mail Stop LC11SA
Olympia, WA 98504

West Virginia CSHCN Program
Division of Handicapped Children's
Services
1116 Quarrier Street
Charleston, WV 25301

Wisconsin CSHCN Program
Division of Handicapped Children
Department of Public Instruction
Bureau for Children with Physical
Needs
P.O. Box 7841
125 South Webster
Madison, WI 53707

Wyoming CSHCN Program
Children's Health Services
Hathaway Building
Cheyenne, WY 82002